Common Core Lessons & Activities:
Mammals

By Carole Marsh

Published by Gallopade International, Inc.

Printed in the U.S.A. (Peachtree City, Georgia)

TABLE OF CONTENTS

G: Includes Graphic Organizer
GO: Graphic Organizer is also available 8½" x 11" online download at www.gallopade.com/client/go
(numbers above correspond to the graphic organizer numbers online)

What Are Mammals?

Read the text and answer the questions.

You see mammals every day—your pet dog or cat, the squirrels scampering in the trees, and even your friends at school. Mammals come in all shapes and sizes, from a tiny 1-inch bat to a giant 90-foot whale. Mammals are the most common form of land animal, but you can find mammals in almost every environment on Earth, including the oceans, caves, and even flying in the air. However, not all animals are mammals. Reptiles, birds, and fish are types of animals that are not mammals.

Fortunately, all mammals have a few important characteristics!

- All mammals are vertebrates (They have a spine).
- All mammals have fur or hair.
- All mammals are warm-blooded.
- All mammal have mammary glands for giving milk to their young.

1. A. List at least three ways mammals can be different from one another.
   B. What four characteristics do all mammals share?
2. An animal that has a spine is called a ______________________.
3. Read the descriptions of each animal. Use the text to identify whether each animal is a mammal. Explain why or why not.

   A. **SEA LION** is a warm-blooded vertebrate that has a shiny, fur coat. It uses flippers to swim in the water and to walk on land. It gives birth to its young and nurses its young with milk for 5-6 months.

   B. **CROCODILE** is a vertebrate that walks on all four legs. It lives on both land and in water. It has rough, leathery skin and is cold-blooded. It lays eggs, and does not give milk to its young.

   C. **RACCOON** is a warm-blooded vertebrate that walks on four legs. It gives birth to its young and nurses its young with milk for 2-3 months.

   D. **BLUE JAYS** are a type of bird. All birds are warm-blooded, have feathers, and have spines. Blue jays lay eggs. When birds hatch, the mother cares for her young, feeding them worms and insects until they are old enough to leave the nest.

Prehistoric Mammals

Read the text and answer the questions.

Mammals are a major part of life on Earth today, but did you know mammals existed during the time of the dinosaurs? The first mammals evolved in the shadows of ferocious dinosaurs that roamed the earth 200 to 65 million years ago.

Scientists have found fossils of mammals dating back to over 200 million years ago. Fossils show that all prehistoric mammals were small and resembled modern-day mice, rats, and other rodents. Fossils also show that the very first prehistoric mammals had some characteristics of reptiles and some characteristics of mammals. Because of this discovery, scientists think that today's mammals might have evolved from prehistoric reptiles.

After the extinction of the dinosaurs, the diversity of mammals greatly increased. Mammals slowly changed over time, grew larger, and spread all around the Earth. Huge prehistoric mammals like Sabertooth Tigers, Mastadons, and Woolly Mammoths roamed the earth from 9 million to 9,000 years ago. Eventually, oversized creatures like the Woolly Mammoth became extinct due to an increasingly warm climate and hunting by modern humans, who appeared about 50,000 years ago.

1. Infer why it might have been advantageous for mammals to be very small when dinosaurs were the dominant form of life.
2. Use the information in the text to order the following events in chronological order:
   _____ The first mammals evolve from prehistoric reptiles.
   _____ The first humans appear.
   _____ Woolly Mammoths become extinct.
   _____ Dinosaurs become extinct.
3. For each effect below, list at least one cause:
   A) The Woolly Mammoth becomes extinct.
   B) The first mammals have several reptile-like characteristics.
   C) Mammals are a very diverse form of life.
   D) Scientists are able to study prehistoric mammals from long ago.
   E) Mammals are a major part of life on Earth.

Classification of Mammals

Read the text, look at the diagram, and answer the questions.

All living organisms are grouped into categories based upon similarities and differences. The broadest category is called a kingdom. The Kingdom Animalia includes all animals. Each category (phylum, class, order, family, genus, and species) below Kingdom is a smaller, more specific group of animals. For example, the Class Mammalia includes all mammals, but the Order Carnivora includes only mammals that eat meat.

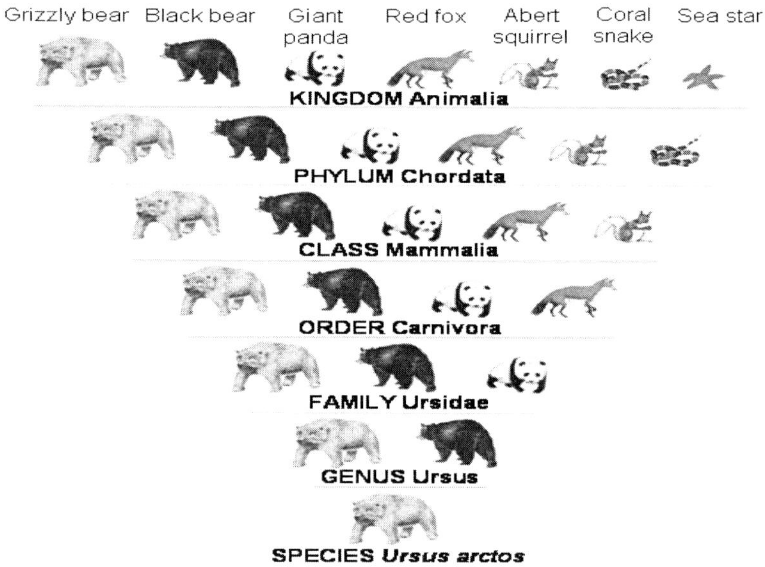

1. Which two animals shown in the diagram are not mammals?
2. Infer what common characteristics the members of the Family Ursidae share. Explain why the Red Fox is not in the Family Ursidae.
3. Use the diagram and make inferences to determine whether each statement is **true** or **false**.
   A. _____ All organisms in the Phylum Chordata are animals.
   B. _____ The Class Mammalia includes the coral snake.
   C. _____ The Abert Squirrel is a mammal that does not eat meat.
   D. _____ The Grizzly Bear and Black Bear are mammals that share the same Family, Genus, and Species.
   E. _____ The Grizzly Bear is more closely related to the Black Bear than to the Red Fox.

Specialized Characteristics

Read the text, look at the pictures, and answer the questions.

Mammals are grouped together by their common characteristics. But, each mammal has differences, called specialized characteristics, that make it unique. Specialized characteristics can help a mammal find food and water in an environment or give protection against predators.

Elephant

Giraffe

Rhinoceros

1. List at least three characteristics that all three mammals have in common

2. A. What specialized characteristics does the elephant have?
   B. Describe how each characteristic might benefit the elephant.

3. A. What specialized characteristics does the giraffe have?
   B. Describe how each characteristic might benefit the giraffe.

4. A. What specialized characteristics does the rhinoceros have?
   B. Describe how each characteristic might benefit the rhinoceros.

5. Read the mammal description below and answer the questions.

I don't have legs like most mammals, but that's just fine. A horse's hooves or a human's skinny arms wouldn't do me any good. My flippers, tail, and fin allow me to swim through the ocean faster than most land mammals can run on land.

I live in the ocean, but I can't breathe water. Luckily, I have a special hole in the top of my head called a blowhole that opens when I need air from the surface. I also have a neat trick called echolocation that helps me find tasty fish.

6. A. Make an educated guess about what mammal is being described.
   B. List at least three specialized characteristics of the mammal.
   C. How do these characteristics suit the mammal to its environment?
   D. Explain why a human or a horse would not be suited to this mammal's environment.

Meeting Basic Needs

Read the text and complete the graphic organizer.

All mammals, including humans, have basic needs they must meet in order to survive. The basic needs of mammals are food, water, and protection.

The place where an animal lives and grows is called its habitat. For most mammals, a habitat provides the water and food the mammal needs to survive. The Giant Panda, for example, primarily eats bamboo. An adult panda can consume around 20 to 45 pounds of bamboo per day. The panda's natural habitat is the bamboo forests of China, where it can find enough bamboo to eat.

Mammals are usually suited to their habitat, meaning they have special characteristics that allow them to find food, water, and protection in their habitat. The striped coat of a Bengal Tiger allows it to hide in its habitat—the jungle. Tigers also have sharp claws and teeth to use when killing and eating animals. The desert might seem like an unlikely habitat for life, but the camel, which stores water in its hump, is perfectly suited to this dry habitat.

1. A. What is the main idea of this text?
2. A. Define habitat as it is used in the text.
   B. List three ways mammals benefit from their habitats. Cite evidence from the text to support your answer.
3. Which dictionary entry below best describes the purpose of a Bengal Tiger's stripes?

A) Deceive — causing someone to believe something untrue
B) Camouflage — To hide or disguise by use of shape or coloring
C) Imitate — To follow or copy a style or way of doing something

4. Explain why the Giant Panda only lives in China.
5. Over many years, the people of China have cut down much of the bamboo forests.
   A. How does bamboo cutting affect the panda's natural habitat?
   B. Predict how bamboo cutting might affect the Giant Panda.

My Needs

Complete the graphic organizer by describing each of your basic needs and how you fulfill those needs. Then read the text and answer the writing prompt.

MEETING MY BASIC NEEDS

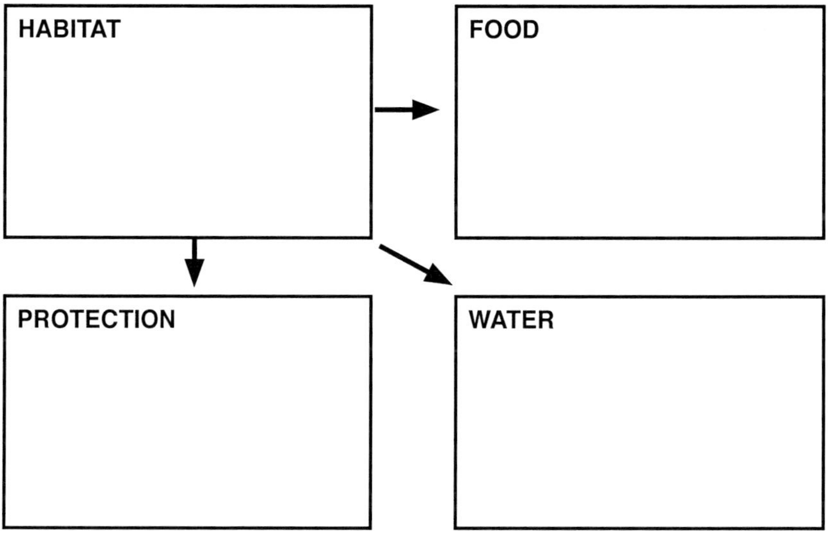

Humans are very complicated mammals. Humans have a higher level of intelligence than any other mammal. To survive in human society, humans need many years of care from parents and many years of education. Humans must learn to solve problems, think creatively, and use many different tools to be successful in life.

Writing Prompt

Answer the following questions in short paragraphs using complete sentences. Draw evidence from your own experience and support your conclusions with logical reasoning.

A. How did your parents/guardian help you meet your basic needs when you were first born?

B. How do they help you meet your basic needs today?

C. What people or groups in your life help you learn and grow?

D. How are you preparing to survive in your “habitat” as in adult?

Mammals and Us

Read the text and answer the questions.

Humans and all other mammals are connected in many ways. For humans, other mammals have many different uses.

Mammals are an important source of food and nutrition. People throughout the world include meat as part of their daily diets. Dairy products like milk and cheese come from mammals. Many jobs are directly related to raising livestock like cattle, sheep, goats, and pigs, all of which are mammals. Many other jobs are related to processing, cooking, and serving meat and dairy products.

Some mammals are cherished and useful to humans. Dogs and cats the most familiar mammals that we keep as pets. Rodent mammals such as guinea pigs and hamsters are also popular pets. Horses are used for sport activities like riding, jumping, and racing. Some mammals like dogs and monkeys are trained to help the elderly and the handicapped. Police teams even use dogs to detect bombs and to search for people who are lost or missing.

Mammals are also an important element in ecosystems we live in. Mammals in the wild are especially important for keeping a balance between predators and prey. For example, wild bobcats help keep deer populations down in many areas. That, in turn, allows woodlands to thrive because deer don't eat too much of the foliage. The presence of trees helps provide the oxygen humans need to survive!

1. Complete the graphic organizer by identifying several ways that mammals affect human lives.

HOW MAMMALS AFFECT HUMAN LIVES

2. List at least five jobs that are directly created as a result of our relationship with mammals. An example is a pet-sitter.

Fur and Hair

Read the text and answer the questions.

Mammals are the ONLY group of animals that has hair or fur. Hair and fur have many functions that benefit mammals.

Insulation Fur and hair keeps mammals warm in cold weather by trapping body heat close to the skin.
Waterproof The fur of some mammals keeps them dry and protects them from losing body heat in cold water.
Camouflage The color or pattern of hair on some mammals allows them to blend in with the natural environment.
Sensing Some animals have special hairs for "sensing" things close to their bodies.
Signaling Special patterns or colors of fur can be used to signal warnings of danger to other mammals, including their prey.
Defense Some mammals have hair that is modified to be sharp. This sharp hair protects the mammal from predators.

1. A. Which functions of hair/fur keep mammals warm?
   B. Which functions of hair/fur protect mammals from harm?
   C. Which functions of hair/fur involve color or pattern?

2. Use the text to identify which function of hair/fur best describes each of the following examples.
   A. ____________ An otter can swim in near-freezing water without its skin getting wet or cold.
   B. ____________ The porcupine may look harmless, but get too close and its prickly spines tell a different story.
   C. ____________ White-tailed deer raise their white tails as a warning sign to other deer when sensing danger.
   D. ____________ Antelope rarely see a cheetah coming until it is too late! A cheetah's yellow and black coloring allows it to disappear in the tall grasses of the African plains.
   E. ____________ When hunting fish, seals use special hair, called whiskers, that allow them to "feel" the movement of fish in the water nearby.
   F. ____________ Polar bears have thick coats of fur that allow them to live in the coldest areas of the Earth!

Keeping Cool & Staying Warm

Read the text and answer the questions.

Staying Warm

Mammals are warm-blooded, which means they produce heat from inside their bodies. Producing body heat takes a lot of energy, because body heat is continuously lost through the skin. In order to stay warm, mammals eat a lot of food for energy. Larger animals typically need more food to keep their larger bodies warm.

Controlling Body Temperature

Mammals have many special characteristics for keeping warm and staying cool. Mammals in different habitats adapt to their environments to control body temperature.

In hot weather, some mammals sweat to cool off. Sweat covers the skin with a layer of water which carries heat away as it evaporates. Some mammals, like dogs, cool off by panting, and cats lick their coats to cause cooling.

In cold weather, mammals' hair and fur traps body heat close to the skin. Polar bears stay warm in freezing temperatures by trapping body heat under layers of fur. Whales keep warm in freezing waters because of a thick layer of fat, called blubber.

A few mammals, including bears, hibernate in the winter to save energy and conserve body heat. In hibernation, a mammal goes into a deep sleep. The mammal's heartbeat, breathing, and life processes slow down to save energy that would have been lost searching for food and staying warm. The mammal survives off fat that it has stored from the summer. When the spring comes, the mammal revives, and continues normal body functioning.

PART A: Use the text to answer the questions.

1. Another word for warm-blooded is endothermic. Choose the correct meaning for the prefix and suffix of this word.

Endo-	a) outside	b) inside	c) adapt
-thermic	a) hibernation	b) energy	c) heat

2. List an advantage and disadvantage of being warm-blooded.
3. Why do most warm-blooded animals eat frequently?

4. List at least four ways that mammals regulate or maintain their body temperatures. Describe the effects of each.

Way of regulating Temperature	Effect

PART B: Look at the table and answer the questions.

AVERAGE FOOD & WATER CONSUMPTION

MAMMAL	AVERAGE WEIGHT	DAILY FOOD CONSUMPTION	DAILY WATER CONSUMPTION
Beluga Whales	1,000 kg	20 kg	50 L
Horses	550 kg	10 kg	60 L
Bottle-nose Dolphins	175 kg	5 kg	11 L
Black Bears	135 kg	4 kg	8 L
Deer	90 kg	3 kg	6 L
Dogs	35 kg	1 kg	3 L
Raccoons	12 kg	530 g	930 mL
River Otters	10 kg	800 g	790 mL
Guinea Pigs	700 g	45 g	65 mL
Gray Squirrels	600 g	45 g	50 mL

Equivalents: 1 kilogram (kg) = 1,000 grams (g); 1 liter (L) = 1,000 milliliters (mL)

5. A. What types of information are shown in this table?
   B. How is the information organized in the table?

6. **True** or **False**: All river otters weigh 10 kg. Explain.

7. A. Describe the relationship between an animal's weight and the amount of food and water it consumes.
   B. What is the reason for this relationship?

8. Explain how and why each of these factors affects how much food a mammal eats:
   A. size B. climate C. hibernation

9. During hibernation, would a black bear's daily food consumption be 4 kg? Explain why or why not.

The Mammal Report

Use at least two online resources to research a mammal of your choice. Take notes and complete the graphic organizer. Highlight facts in the graphic organizer that are characteristics of all mammals. Then do the "Guess the Mammal" activity.

Physical Characteristics

My Mammal:

Reproductive & Care of Young

Behavioral Adaptations

Guess the Mammal

PART A: Use your research to write a first-person description of your mammal. Do not reveal the name of your mammal! Be sure to include enough clues to identify your mammal. Be creative!

PART B: Read your first-person description aloud to your class. Can your classmates accurately identify your mammal from your description?

Habitat

Other Interesting Facts

A Bite to Eat

Read the text and answer the questions.

Scientists often categorize mammals into four categories based on what they eat. Insectivores, as their name suggests, eat insects. Herbivores primarily eat plants. Carnivores mostly eat meat. Omnivores eat both plants and meat. Mammals in each group have special characteristics based on the way they find, capture, chew, swallow, and digest food. Two of the main characteristics are digestive systems and teeth.

Digestive System

A mammal's digestive system changes nutrients from food into energy. Insectivores, carnivores, and omnivores have simple, shorter digestive systems which process food quickly. Herbivores have longer, more complex digestive systems because plant matter is hard to digest and get nutrients from. There are two types of herbivores: ruminant and non-ruminant. A non-ruminant herbivore grazes all day long, eating huge quantities of food but getting very little nutrients from it. Ruminant herbivores do not eat as often because ruminant herbivores digest their food twice, getting more nutrients from the plants.

Teeth

Mammals also have specialized teeth depending on the food they eat. There are four different types of mammal teeth—incisors, canines, premolars, and molars.

Carnivores have sharp incisors and canines that help them tear meat from the bones of their prey. The molars and premolars of canines are also sharp and used for cutting and chewing meat. Insectivores have long incisors that help them grasp tiny bugs from deep holes. The canines of herbivores are usually smaller and look like wedges. A cow uses its wedge-like canines and incisors to cut through grasses and leaves. The molars and premolars of herbivores are often flat and rounded for grinding plant matter.

Because the teeth of mammals reflect their eating habits, scientists can make an educated guess about what a mammal eats by looking at its teeth!

1. The suffix "-vore" means "to eat" and is used to describe the diet of a specific animal. Make inferences from the text to explain the meaning of each prefix.

Prefix	Meaning
Insecti-	
Herbi-	
Carni-	
Omni-	

2. Based on what you eat, which word best classifies you—insectivore, carnivore, herbivore, or omnivore? Explain why.
3. Which category of mammals most likely spends a lot of time:
   A. hunting B. digging in the earth C. grazing
4. An animal with sharp front canines and rounded back molars is most likely which category of mammal?
5. What can a mammal's teeth tell us about its digestive system? Cite evidence from the text to explain how.
6. Compare and contrast the two mammal skulls and answer the questions below.

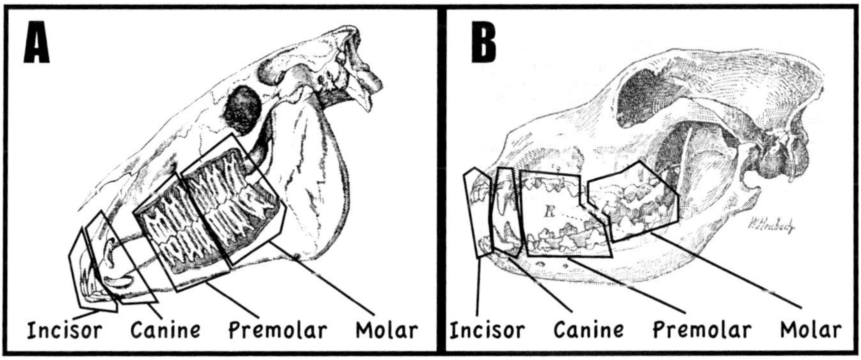

A. Compare diagram A and diagram B and list the similarities and differences in each type of tooth.
B. Describe the function of each type of tooth in each diagram based upon its shape.
C. Infer what category of mammal is shown in Diagram A. Explain.
D. Infer what category of mammal is shown in Diagram B. Explain.
E. Explain how scientists might use differences in a mammal's teeth to classify mammals into different categories.

Types of Mammals

Read the text and answer the questions.

All mammals fall into one of three types based upon how they give birth to their young.

Most mammals, including humans, are placental mammals. Placental mammals are mammals that have a placenta. This organ provides food and oxygen to a baby inside the mother's womb. The baby grows and completes its development inside the mother over a period of time called gestation. Placental mammals give birth to live babies. Placental mammals can be found in environments around the world. Placental mammals range from rodents like squirrels and mice to monkeys, horses, and dogs, to bats, elephants, and even whales and dolphins.

Marsupials are mammals that carry their young in a pouch. Marsupials have a very short gestation, which does not give their young time to fully grow. After giving birth, a marsupial mammal carries its young in a protective pouch. Through the pouch, the mother gives milk and other nutrients to its young until it is ready to leave the pouch. Most marsupials are found in Australia and New Zealand, including koalas, kangaroos, wallabies, and cuscus. The opossum is one of the few marsupials that live in North America.

Monotremes are mammals that lay eggs. All other mammals give birth to live babies, but the monotreme lays eggs. Monotremes are the smallest category of mammals. In fact, there are only two groups of monotremes: the Duck-billed Platypus and the echidnas. Monotremes are also different in another way—they have lower body temperatures, like reptiles. However, monotremes are classified as mammals because they have hair and feed their babies with mother's milk. Platypuses and echidnas are found only in Australia, Tasmania, and New Guinea.

PART A: Use the text to complete the table.

Word	Part of Speech	Definition
placenta		
gestation		

PART B: Summarize information from the text to compare and contrast monotremes, marsupials, and placental mammals.

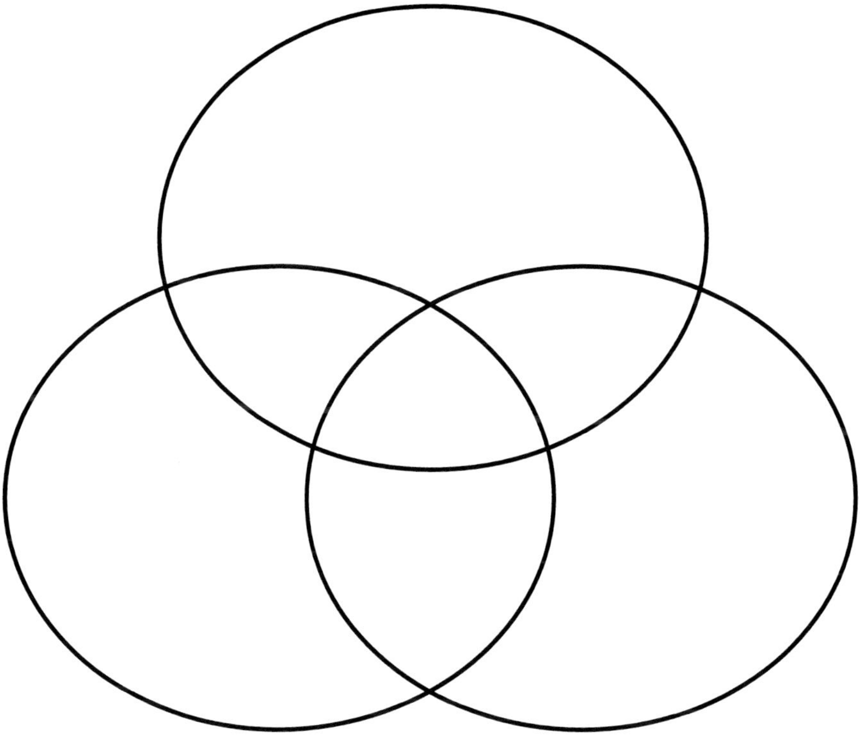

PART C: Determine whether each statement is a **fact (F)** or **opinion (O)**.

1. _____ Mammals can be classified based on how their young are born.
2. _____ Placental, marsupial, and monotreme are logical categories.
3. _____ Most mammals are in the placental category.
4. _____ The placental mammal category should be divided into smaller categories because it is so large.
5. _____ Marsupials are interesting because they have a pouch.
6. _____ Marsupial babies are less developed than placental babies when born.
7. _____ Monotremes should not be categorized as mammals because they lay eggs like a bird.
8. _____ Monotremes are classified as mammals because they have hair and feed their babies mother's milk.

Caring for Their Young

Read the text and answer the questions.

All mammal mothers have glands called mammary glands that produce milk to feed their young. Milk provides nutrients for the young mammal until it grows old enough to eat other foods. Because a young mammal needs nutrients from its mother's milk, it is closely connected to its mother during its early life.

Besides providing nutrients to their young, mammal parents also teach their young important skills to help them survive later in life. Mammals are able to learn skills, recognize patterns, and solve problems. Mammal parents teach their young basic skills like how to find food or how to find shelter.

Some types of mammals live in groups and teach their young the rules of the group. For example, one male lion called the "alpha male" makes the rules for the whole pride of lions. Wolves and elephants often have leaders, too. A mammal that does not follow the group's rules is often sent away from the group.

Mammals that live in groups also teach their young to cooperate. Some mammals, like lions and wolves, cooperate by hunting together to catch food more easily. Some mammals, like elephants, cooperate in groups to protect against predators.

1. A. Define mammary glands as it is used in the text.
   B. How do mammary glands benefit mammals?
2. Read each statement and explain the benefit to the young mammal.
   A. Mammal young learn basic skills from their parents.
   B. Mammal young learn the rules of the group.
   C. Mammal young learn to cooperate.
3. A. Why is it important to follow rules in a group? Give an example from your own experience.
   B. List at least 5 ways that humans cooperate with each other.
4. In general, mammals have very few young at one time. Propose a hypothesis to explain why mammals have very few young at one time. Cite evidence from the text to support your hypothesis. As a class, discuss your hypotheses and explain how they might be tested.

CLASSIFYING INFORMATION

Placental Orders

Look at the table and answer the questions.

Placental mammals are the largest category of mammals. Scientists have divided it into smaller categories called orders.

Order Name	Examples	Characteristics
Artiodactyla	Deer, sheep, pigs, antelopes	Plant eaters, hooves, even number of toes
Carnivora	Dogs, cats, bears, otters, seals	Meat eaters, teeth for tearing flesh
Cetacea	Dolphins, whales	Blowholes, only front limbs, flippers
Chiroptera	Bats	Fruit and insect eaters, nocturnal, flyers, use sonar
Insectivora	Shrews, hedgehogs	Insect eaters, pointed snouts, live underground
Lagomorpha	Rabbits, pikas	Front teeth that continuously grow, back legs longer than front legs
Perissodactyla	Horses, zebras, rhinoceroses	Plant eaters, hooves, odd number of toes
Primates	Monkeys, apes, humans	Large brains, opposable thumbs, binocular vision
Proboscidea	Elephants	Long trunks, front teeth that become tusks
Rodentia	Beavers, rats, guinea pigs	Plant eaters, sharp front teeth
Sirenia	Manatees	Large heads, only front limbs, flippers, slow moving
Xenarthra	Anteaters, sloths, armadillos	Insect eaters, toothless or peg-like teeth

1. A. What is an order?

   B. List at least five types of mammal characteristics that scientists use to classify mammals.

2. List two pairs of orders that share at least one characteristic.

3. Use the table to identify the order each mammal belongs to.

   A. __________ A mole is a small insect-eating mammal. It digs in the earth and makes underground burrows to live in.

   B. ___________ A goat can often be seen grazing on grass and other plants. Like a horse, goats have hooves, but unlike a horse, goats have an even number of toes.

   C. ___________ A lion is one of the most feared animals on Earth because it has sharp claws and sharp teeth for eating meat.

   D ___________ Squirrels have sharp front teeth for eating nuts.

Endangered and Extinct

Read the text and answer the questions.

When the last animal of a species dies, the species is extinct. The dinosaur and dodo bird are examples of animals that no longer exist. Throughout Earth's history, many species have become extinct. Additionally, there are many species whose populations are so low, they are at risk of becoming extinct. These endangered species, such as the bald eagle, could become extinct very soon.

Sometimes extinction is a natural process. For example, mammals may become extinct because of widespread disease, a volcanic eruption, flooding, or severe drought.

Sometimes extinction occurs because of actions by humans. In order to get natural resources, such as lumber, and to clear land for growing cities, humans have cut down forests faster than trees can grow. This deforestation destroys the habitat that many mammals depend on to survive. Pollution from cars, businesses, and homes can poison the land, water, and air that many mammals need to survive. Over-hunting can also leave mammal populations very small. For example, rhinoceroses have been killed for their horns, and are now extremely endangered.

1. A. Use the text to define extinct and endangered.
   B. Describe the relationship between endangered and extinct.
   C. List four natural events that can cause extinction.
2. A. Use the text to define deforestation.
   B. Why does deforestation occur?
3. For each cause, list a direct effect that can lead to extinction.
   A. Deforestation B. Pollution C. Over-hunting
4. A. Use an online resource to research an endangered animal. Learn what is being done to prevent it from becoming extinct. Describe who is involved, the efforts they are making, the problems they face, and the success they have had. Predict whether they will succeed or fail and cite evidence from your research to support your prediction.
   B. Summarize your research and prediction into a poster presentation or a digital slideshow. Include visuals.
   C. Present your poster or slideshow to your class.

PROBLEM-SOLUTION-RESULTS

Fighting Mammal Extinction

Complete the graphic organizer to propose a solution for one or more of the following problems threatening mammals.

Deforestation **Pollution** **Over-hunting**

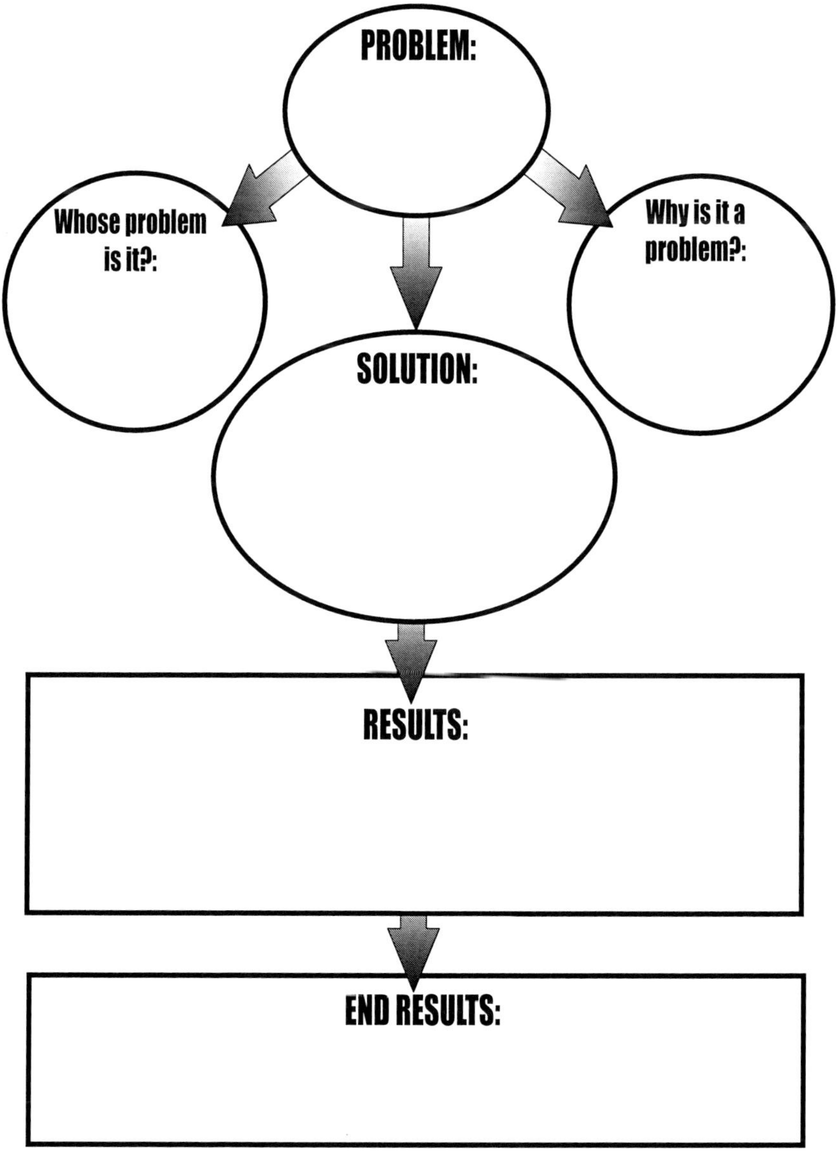

PRIMARY SOURCE ANALYSIS

The Wise Platypus

Read the story and answer the questions.

The Tale of the Wise Platypus

In the Dreamtime at the Earth's beginning, every group of animals thought itself special. These groups would gather for meetings to discuss how unique they were from all other creatures.

The birds talked of how they had feathers, they could fly, and they laid eggs. The mammals discussed their fur and their ability to run across the land. The sea creatures talked of their ability to swim and their unique underwater home.

But Platypus did not attend any of these meetings. Eventually, a representative from each special group asked Platypus to join their meetings.

Platypus listened to each creature. Then she asked them all to leave her so she could think about their offers. She talked with her family and her friend, Echidna. Finally, she asked the other animals to return to hear her decision. They gathered around her home and she climbed onto a log to speak to them. "Thank you for coming today," she began. "I have decided not to join any group at all."

The other creatures were shocked! "You must join someone's group!" they cried.

Platypus continued, "After thinking long and hard, I realized that I am special just as I am. I don't need to join a group to prove that. I have fur like my mammal friends, I lay eggs like my bird friends, and I share a love of water with my sea creature friends. We are alike in many ways. But, I am also different from each of you. Those differences don't make me better than you, just like your special qualities don't make you better than me. Every one of us is unique in our own way and each of us is truly one-of-a-kind."

All the creatures agreed, and from that time forward, Platypus was seen as wise and very special indeed.

1. The purpose of this story is to:
   A. teach a moral B. persuade your opinion C. give scientific facts
2. Who do you think is the intended audience of this story? Why?
3. Personification is the act of giving human characteristics to non-human things. Describe the use of personification in the story.
4. A. What typical mammal characteristic does the platypus have?
   B. What platypus characteristics are unusual for a mammal?
5. A. What is the main message of the story?
   B. Do you agree or disagree with the message? Why or why not?

Mammal Vocabulary

Use what you have learned and a dictionary to write a definition for each vocabulary word. For each group of words, write a title that describes that group of words.

Title: Mammal Characteristics

Vocabulary	Definition
fur/ hair	
mammary gland	
vertebrate	
warm-blooded	

Title:

Vocabulary	Definition
carnivore	
herbivore	
insectivore	
omnivore	

Title:

Vocabulary	Definition
marsupial	
monotreme	
placental mammal	

Title:

Vocabulary	Definition
extinct	
fossil	
prehistoric	

Correlations to Common Core State Standards

For your convenience, correlations are listed page-by-page, and for the entire book!

This book is correlated to the Common Core State Standards for English Language Arts grades 3-8, and to Common Core State Standards for Literacy in History, Science, & Technological Subjects grades 6-8.

Correlations are highlighted in gray.

PAGE #	READING *Includes:* RI: Reading Informational Text RST: Reading Science & Technical Subjects	WRITING *Includes:* W: Writing WHST: Writing History/Social Studies, Science, & Technical Subjects	LANGUAGE *Includes:* L: Language LF: Language Foundational Skills	SPEAKING & LISTENING *Includes:* SL: Speaking & Listening
2	RI RST . 1 2 3 4 5 6 7 8 9 10	W WHST . 1 2 3 4 5 6 7 8 9 10	L LF . 1 2 3 4 5 6	SL . 1 2 3 4 5 6
3	RI RST . 1 2 3 4 5 6 7 8 9 10	W WHST . 1 2 3 4 5 6 7 8 9 10	L LF . 1 2 3 4 5 6	SL . 1 2 3 4 5 6
4	RI RST . 1 2 3 4 5 6 7 8 9 10	W WHST . 1 2 3 4 5 6 7 8 9 10	L LF . 1 2 3 4 5 6	SL . 1 2 3 4 5 6
5	RI RST . 1 2 3 4 5 6 7 8 9 10	W WHST . 1 2 3 4 5 6 7 8 9 10	L LF . 1 2 3 4 5 6	SL . 1 2 3 4 5 6
6	RI RST . 1 2 3 4 5 6 7 8 9 10	W WHST . 1 2 3 4 5 6 7 8 9 10	L LF . 1 2 3 4 5 6	SL . 1 2 3 4 5 6
7	RI RST . 1 2 3 4 5 6 7 8 9 10	W WHST . 1 2 3 4 5 6 7 8 9 10	L LF . 1 2 3 4 5 6	SL . 1 2 3 4 5 6
8	RI RST . 1 2 3 4 5 6 7 8 9 10	W WHST . 1 2 3 4 5 6 7 8 9 10	L LF . 1 2 3 4 5 6	SL . 1 2 3 4 5 6
9	RI RST . 1 2 3 4 5 6 7 8 9 10	W WHST . 1 2 3 4 5 6 7 8 9 10	L LF . 1 2 3 4 5 6	SL . 1 2 3 4 5 6
10-11	RI RST . 1 2 3 4 5 6 7 8 9 10	W WHST . 1 2 3 4 5 6 7 8 9 10	L LF . 1 2 3 4 5 6	SL . 1 2 3 4 5 6
12-13	RI RST . 1 2 3 4 5 6 7 8 9 10	W WHST . 1 2 3 4 5 6 7 8 9 10	L LF . 1 2 3 4 5 6	SL . 1 2 3 4 5 6
14-15	RI RST . 1 2 3 4 5 6 7 8 9 10	W WHST . 1 2 3 4 5 6 7 8 9 10	L LF . 1 2 3 4 5 6	SL . 1 2 3 4 5 6
16-17	RI RST . 1 2 3 4 5 6 7 8 9 10	W WHST . 1 2 3 4 5 6 7 8 9 10	L LF . 1 2 3 4 5 6	SL . 1 2 3 4 5 6
18	RI RST . 1 2 3 4 5 6 7 8 9 10	W WHST . 1 2 3 4 5 6 7 8 9 10	L LF . 1 2 3 4 5 6	SL . 1 2 3 4 5 6
19	RI RST . 1 2 3 4 5 6 7 8 9 10	W WHST . 1 2 3 4 5 6 7 8 9 10	L LF . 1 2 3 4 5 6	SL . 1 2 3 4 5 6
20	RI RST . 1 2 3 4 5 6 7 8 9 10	W WHST . 1 2 3 4 5 6 7 8 9 10	L LF . 1 2 3 4 5 6	SL . 1 2 3 4 5 6
21	RI RST . 1 2 3 4 5 6 7 8 9 10	W WHST . 1 2 3 4 5 6 7 8 9 10	L LF . 1 2 3 4 5 6	SL . 1 2 3 4 5 6
22	RI RST . 1 2 3 4 5 6 7 8 9 10	W WHST . 1 2 3 4 5 6 7 8 9 10	L LF . 1 2 3 4 5 6	SL . 1 2 3 4 5 6
23	RI RST . 1 2 3 4 5 6 7 8 9 10	W WHST . 1 2 3 4 5 6 7 8 9 10	L LF . 1 2 3 4 5 6	SL . 1 2 3 4 5 6
COMPLETE BOOK	RI RST 1 2 3 4 5 6 7 8 9 10	W WHST 1 2 3 4 5 6 7 8 9 10	L LF 1 2 3 4 5 6	SL . 1 2 3 4 5 6

For the complete Common Core standard identifier, combine your grade + "." + letter code above + "." + number code above.

In addition to the correlations indicated here, the activities may be adapted or expanded to align to additional standards and to meet the diverse needs of your unique students!